Thirty & Thriving

A guided adventure journal to help you live your 30th year boldly
and with no regrets

Krystal Speed

Printed in the United States of America

First Printing, 2020

ISBN 978-1-7346477-0-9

www.krystalspeed.com

*To all the sisters out there, bold enough and brave enough to go on this year of adventures - this journal is dedicated to you! Honey, I am SO proud of you.
Do your thang!*

HAPPY 30TH BIRTHDAY!!!

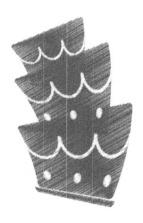

Table of Contents

Directions: Check off each item as you complete it. Enjoy the adventure!

Introduction

Girl. Get. It.

You are 30 & you are thriving. It's time to celebrate you - ALL YEAR LONG!

Personally, I am a fan of birthdays - whether it's mine or someone else's! Birthdays can be incredible. And milestone birthdays, well they are something extra special to celebrate. Some throw the party on their actual birth date. Others may take a week to do different things with family and friends to mark the occasion. Still, others claim the entire month as their own.

Guess what, Boo! Right now, we are declaring the whole year is YOURS. It is time to celebrate, explore and make meaningful memories this year! Live it up! You only turn 30 once.

I mean, turning 30 is no small thing. It's usually around this age that people start feeling grown, for real, lol. You may finally have the bomb career, for which you've worked so long and so hard. Perhaps, you are in THE right relationship that you've always desired. Maybe not everything has fallen into place, but you know where you are now is where you are meant to be. Because of these things, and so much more, you are ready to thrive in your 30s. That, my dear, is worth celebrating!

This year I challenge you to try new things, connect with past joys and explore the world around you. This journal will be your adventure companion as you record and reflect upon the 30 things you are doing to celebrate your 30th year.

Now, don't overthink it. Just identify 30 things you want to do this year. Then, do them! They can be simple, like enjoy an uninterrupted bubble bath (mommas, I'm talking to you). Try a new ice cream flavor - see that? It doesn't have to break the bank...unless you want to go big. And, why not? You may decide to use some of those extra coins you've saved up to take that long-awaited dream vacation.

Whatever you decide to do, just do it with a spirit of boldness and adventure. Go with an open heart and open mind and see what happens. Some things you will absolutely love! Others you'll never want to do again. Both are fine. It's about the process of living life with no regrets, trying new things and learning more about you and the world around you in the process.

Let me tell you how this year of adventure works. This journal has enough space for you to capture details about each of the 30 experiences you intentionally seek out during this 30th year of life. Here's what you're going to do:

- **Select 30 experiences to pursue this year.** Don't worry. You don't need to pick all 30 today. Take your time and as a brilliant idea hits you, jot it down. I provided some examples earlier. If you need more inspiration, check out **More Celebration Ideas** at the end of this journal. They are general ideas to help ignite your creativity.

- **Plan your experience.** Since you will complete 30 experiences this year, each one is numbered in your journal. Use the line directly under the number to write out what you will do. No need for a lot of words - be specific and concise. Example: Go snow tubing with the crew on Jan. 25th.

- **After you complete the experience, write about it.** Each adventure has 2 pages, ample space for you to recount all the details of what you did. There are no rules here- just write, draw, attach photos, insert a ticket stub - whatever you want. Consider including details that you don't want to forget - where you went, how you felt doing the activity, names of those who joined you or that you met, etc. You may also find it helpful to jot down if it is something you definitely want to do again or if it was a "one-and-done" type of situation.

Simple, right?!

In this journal, you'll also find 2 prompts where you are encouraged to write a letter to yourself. The first letter is designed to be completed when you start this year of bold living. Be honest with yourself with how you feel about turning 30. Share the good, the bad, the ugly. It's just for you.

The other letter is to be written when you finish. It serves as a check-in and celebration point after you finish your year of fab 50 adventures. See how you've changed and dream about what you may want to conquer next.

One final thing. Don't forget to share with everyone all the fun you have this year! As you share on your social posts, use **#thirty&thrivingjournal**. I can't wait to see what you're up to and I'll be sure to show you some love. As a person that loves trying new things, I'm definitely looking forward to trying out some of *your* fab50 celebration experiences myself.

Now, go make some fab memories! Enjoy the journey! Love, laugh and live boldly because you are 30, and you are thriving!

Cupcakes & Cheers!

Krystal

Happy Birthday
Beautiful!

Happy Birthday Beautiful!

It's your birthday! Today is your day. Mark this special day by showing yourself some love. What better way, than to write yourself a letter? Use these pages to reflect upon how you feel, what you've learned these last 29 years and what you are looking forward to this year and beyond. Take a moment to love on your beautiful self.

_____

_____

_____

_____

_____

_____

_____

_____

_____

_____

_____

Let the Adventures Begin!

Adventure 1

The Experience

Adventure 2

The Experience

_____

_____

_____

_____

_____

_____

_____

_____

_____

_____

_____

Adventure 3

The Experience

_____

_____

_____

_____

_____

_____

_____

_____

_____

_____

_____

Adventure 4

The Experience

Adventure 5

The Experience

_____

_____

_____

_____

_____

_____

_____

_____

_____

_____

Adventure 6

The Experience

_____
_____
_____
_____
_____
_____
_____
_____
_____
_____
_____
_____

Adventure 7

The Experience

_____

_____

_____

_____

_____

_____

_____

_____

_____

_____

_____

Adventure 8

The Experience

_____

_____

_____

_____

_____

_____

_____

_____

_____

_____

_____

Adventure 9

The Experience

_____

_____

_____

_____

_____

_____

_____

_____

_____

_____

Adventure 10

The Experience

Adventure 11

The Experience

Adventure 12

The Experience

_____

_____

_____

_____

_____

_____

_____

_____

_____

_____

_____

_____

Adventure 13

The Experience

_____

_____

_____

_____

_____

_____

_____

_____

_____

_____

_____

_____

Adventure 14

The Experience

Adventure 15

The Experience

_____
_____
_____
_____
_____
_____
_____
_____
_____
_____
_____

Adventure 16

The Experience

Adventure 17

The Experience

_____

_____

_____

_____

_____

_____

_____

_____

_____

_____

Adventure 18

The Experience

_____

_____

_____

_____

_____

_____

_____

_____

_____

_____

Adventure 19

The Experience

Adventure 20

The Experience

_____

_____

_____

_____

_____

_____

_____

_____

_____

_____

Adventure 21

The Experience

Adventure 22

The Experience

Adventure 23

The Experience

Adventure 24

The Experience

_____

_____

_____

_____

_____

_____

_____

_____

_____

_____

_____

Adventure 25

The Experience

_____

_____

_____

_____

_____

_____

_____

_____

_____

_____

Adventure 26

The Experience

Adventure 27

The Experience

_____

_____

_____

_____

_____

_____

_____

_____

_____

Adventure 28

The Experience

_____

_____

_____

_____

_____

_____

_____

_____

_____

_____

Adventure 29

The Experience

_____

_____

_____

_____

_____

_____

_____

_____

_____

_____

Adventure 30

The Experience

_____

_____

_____

_____

_____

_____

_____

_____

_____

_____

_____

_____

_____

Girl, Thrive!

Girl, Thrive!

You did it. How do you feel? Did you accomplish all you wanted? Is there more you desire? What surprised you this year? In what ways did you fall back or deeper in love with a part of yourself? Let it all out on these pages as you write a letter to yourself celebrating all you've experienced!

_____

_____

_____

_____

_____

_____

_____

_____

_____

_____

_____

_____

_____

More Celebration Ideas

More Celebration Ideas

Stuck? Here are some general ideas that you can customize and try this year.

- Try a new food.
- Book that solo trip.
- Recreate a favorite childhood memory.
- Pick up a hobby from your past.
- Go see a play.
- Try out a new, bold, color (hair, nails, lipstick, piece of clothing).
- Check out a local festival.
- Write a book.
- Take some "me time".
- Enjoy a night of karaoke with friends.
- Try a new fitness activity or sport.
- Host a game night with friends.
- Go on a hot date (new beau, husband, kids, parents).
- Be a local tourist for the day/weekend.
- Reconnect with your roots/heritage.
- Host a dinner party.
- Travel internationally.
- Treat yourself to a date on the town.
- Enroll in a class.
- Host a friend for the day/weekend.
- Call or write a letter to say thank you to someone that had a significant impact on your life.
- Plan a first-time visit to a new US city.
- Read a book from an unfamiliar author.
- Volunteer or give back to your community.
- Go for high tea.
- Buy some stock.

Made in United States
North Haven, CT
14 December 2022

28676634R00049